# Jesus in Our Days

# Divaldo Franco
## by the Spirit Joanna de Ângelis

# Jesus in Our Days

LEAL Publisher

Copyright© 2016 by
Centro Espírita Caminho da Redenção – Salvador (BA) – Brazil

All rights reserved. No part of this book may be reproduced by any mechanical, photographic, or electronic process, or in the form of a phonographic recording; nor may it be stored in a retrieval system, transmitted, or otherwise be copied for public or private use without prior written permission of the publisher.

ISBN: 978-1-942408-15-4

Original title in Portuguese:
*Jesus e Atualidade*
(Brazil, 1989)

Translated by: Darrel W. Kimble and Claudia Dealmeida
Cover design by: Cláudio Urpia
Layout: Luciano Carneiro Holanda
Edited by: Evelyn Yuri Furuta

Edition of
LEAL PUBLISHER
8425 Biscayne Blvd. Suite 104
Miami, Florida 33138, USA
www.lealpublisher.com
info@lealpublisher.com
(305) 306-6447

Authorized edition by Centro Espírita Caminho da Redenção – Salvador (BA) – Brazil

INTERNATIONAL DATA FOR CATALOGING IN PUBLICATION (ICP)

| | |
|---|---|
| f825 | Ângelis, de Joanna (Spirit). *Jesus in Our Days* / authored by the Spirit Joanna de Ângelis; psychographed by Divaldo Pereira Franco ; translated by Darrel Kimble and Claudia Dealmeida – Miami (FL), USA : Leal Publisher, 2016. 90 p. ; 21 cm |
| | Original title: Jesus e Atualidade |
| | ISBN 978-1-942408-15-4 |
| | 1. Spiritism. 2. Jesus. 3. Psychology I. Franco, Divaldo Pereira, 1927-. II. Title. CDD 133.9 CDU 133.7 |

# Contents

Jesus in Our Days ..................................................7
1. Jesus and Challenges ........................................11
2. Jesus and Reincarnation ...................................15
3. Jesus and Humanity ........................................19
4. Jesus and Love ................................................23
5. Jesus and Tolerance .........................................27
6. Jesus and Honor ..............................................31
7. Jesus and Justice ..............................................35
8. Jesus and Duty ................................................39
9. Jesus and Joy ...................................................43
10. Jesus and Courage .........................................47
11. Jesus and Resolve ..........................................51
12. Jesus and Responsibility ................................55
13. Jesus and Revolution .....................................59
14. Jesus and Possessions ....................................63
15. Jesus and Torments .......................................67
16. Jesus and Rest ...............................................71
17. Jesus and Insecurity ......................................75
18. Jesus and Suffering .......................................79
19. Jesus and Ingratitude ....................................83
20. Jesus and Enemies ........................................87

# Jesus in Our Days

*I*n our day, the timeliness of Jesus' thinking impresses even the most skeptical scholars of the always complex and challenging human condition.

With a profound understanding of the psyche,[1] Jesus confidently probed the innermost recesses of the individual and discovered the real causes of the afflictions that the unconscious was trying to hide.

Without distractions or delays, He confronted issues with a high level of wisdom, which laid bare the most intricate psychopathological personalities, proposing a rigorously compatible therapy, emphasizing personal responsibility and eliminating the projected shadow, under which many lay hidden.

Using more time-consuming processes, in-depth psychology has arrived at the same results that He so easily achieved two thousand years ago.

Roberto Assagioli, for example, with his psychosynthesis, reached down into the causes of various diseases and concluded

---

[1] (*Psychiatry*) The mind functioning as the center of thought, emotion, and behavior and consciously or unconsciously adjusting or mediating the body›s responses to the social and physical environment. http://www.thefreedictionary.com – Tr.

*that the "transpersonal" reality of the individual was the triggering factor.*

*Abraham Maslow discovered the "psychology of being" and paved the way for the profound understanding of the psychogenesis of the diseases that damage the human personality.*

*Groff, linking the mind with the brain, went further and confronted the immortal being as the agent of countless psychopathologies.*

*Concerning schizophrenics, the Freudians Melanie Klein and Carl Johnson proposed therapy based on love, charity and Christian forgiveness as the most effective, even though they themselves were not religious.*

*Jesus' remarkable personality indelibly impressed everyone who met Him.*

*At one with God, Jesus manifested Him at every step, exhorting His listeners to seek the ultimate reality – the Kingdom of Heaven – which lies within each individual.*

*His proposal for assessing values – the material along with the spiritual – offered an excellent opportunity for mental awakening regarding life and its consequent experiences in an atmosphere of inner harmony, discriminating between one's abilities and the existential circumstances.*

*Avoiding interpolated expressions and concepts, He spoke with simplicity to the ignorant masses and the elite minds that sought Him out.*

*An extraordinary storyteller – one of the most difficult arts in the area of discourse – and an unparalleled poet due to the pure images, rich in color and meaning, His teachings became timeless, recognized as the most beautiful ever recorded by gnosis.*

*The Sermon on the Mount, considered the "Magna Carta of Human Rights," is a challenge of nonviolence, as apropos for the present time as it was for the time in which He enunciated it. Those who heard Him would be forever pervaded with its incomparable magic.*

*However, Jesus is not only current due to His therapy of love and the lessons He offers to contemporary men and women, but also on account of the very picture of the beatitude and peace He radiated.*

*While unbridled ambition drives people to paroxysm and the illusion of possession, fame, glory, and blind competition, He fully resurfaces, jovial and friendly, in the modern human consciousness, beatified by His humanitarian nature and self-confidence.*

*The present desperately needs an uncrucified Jesus, a companion and therapist offering urgent assistance to keep it from going over the edge.*

*With this pressing issue in mind, we decided to write this little book, addressing twenty contemporary situations entailing everyday circumstances that trouble civilization. It provides behavioral guidelines based on Jesus' therapy, the results of which are obviously health, peace and happiness as experiences not yet enjoyed individually or collectively.*

*Certain that our dear readers will find in these pages answers to a few personal concerns, we implore Him to guide and sustain us on our way as we eagerly pursue complete realization.*

JOANNA DE ÂNGELIS
Salvador, Brazil, February 20, 1989

# 1
# JESUS AND CHALLENGES

The process of evolution is a tremendous challenge for the spirit.

Accustomed to the powerful sensations of the physical senses, only when pain pays a visit does the spirit begin to aspire to higher emotions in which to find solace, and long for greater achievements.

Living in constant struggle against the constraints of its current evolutionary level, only occasionally does the spirit experience peace, which it wants to last forever.

At the start, the spirit coexists with pain, interrupted by brief episodes of wellness, until it finds tranquility, interrupted by brief episodes of pain. Ultimately, it experiences joy uninterrupted.

Step by step, it ascends, falls down and gets up again, attracted by the sublime tropism of Love.

Reaching the summit means victory.

Shaken and insecure, the spirit *discovers* a widespread conspiracy against its destiny. Its legacy from the past now reappears and tries to retain it in the restrictive area of immediacy, on a lower level of consciousness, where eating, sleeping and reproducing are all that matter. It is indifferent to the emotions of the beautiful, the noble, the wholesome.

Anesthetized by such vegetative needs, it seeks only pleasure, which ultimately saturates it, and it moves on to the boredom that precedes the pressing need for something better.

It slowly awakens to once meaningless realities that now suddenly become a desired goal, and it feels encouraged to abandon its idleness.

Its latent Divine Consciousness responds to this higher appeal by freeing itself of its cellular prison, like an antenna capturing only the messages to which it is attuned.

The first challenge – that of experiencing new emotions – attracts it, urging it onward to increasingly more complex and audacious endeavors.

As it experiences this ethical and aesthetic pleasure, so different from its earlier animality, it becomes accustomed to it and strives for new commitments that, henceforth, never cease, since, like an infinite spiral, once a cycle is over, another more attractive and seemingly more easily attainable one opens up.

Everything in life is an endurance test.

The Law of Entropy degrades energy, which tends toward consumption in order to maintain thermodynamic balance in all things.

Aging and death are unavoidable phenomena both in the biological cosmos and in the universe.

Heartbeats are challenges for the muscle that experiences them; peristaltic waves are a continuous test for the fibers that endure them; blood circulation is an essential process for the irrigation of the cells; breathing is a vital function, without which life ceases. All this and much more in the area of physiological automatisms affect our psychological nature.

It is only natural that the same happens in the moral arena of the individual, who never regresses and must never remain stationary – for any reason.

In terms of progress, evolution is unavoidable.

Bliss is the ultimate destination.

✶

One must not retreat in battle, except to refuel in order to press on.

The growth of any ideal results from lower stages overcome and challenges met.

The giant sequoia reaches maximum height and girth cell by cell.

The universe renews and perpetuates itself molecule by molecule.

Too easy a task is a danger to motivation and hinders one's action.

The Master's entire life was a constant succession of challenges.

Obstacles in His social and family environment were His first impediments, which He overcame for the sake of the ultimate purpose for which He had come.

He did not consent to carry the world's burden as redemption for others. Instead, He taught that one should carry one's own encumbrance with a peaceful conscience. He did not assume others' responsibilities. Rather, He showed how to go about them without presumption or cowardly submission.

In an unjust and arbitrary society, situations, persons and circumstances challenged Him; even so, without holding back, He kept His integrity and faced them without anger or fear.

That time has passed; the sickly vestiges, however, remain.

The landscape has changed, but not the values; they are still the same, generating obstacles and dissatisfaction.

Serenely face the challenges of your own life.

Do not wait for comforts that you do not deserve.

Proceed on your journey bravely, preserving your inner values and strengthening them through daily practice.

Those who fear the darkness get lost in the night.

Be someone who lights up a candle to chase away the darkness.

Challenged, Jesus prevailed. Follow Him and never hold back before the tests meant for your spiritual growth.

# 2
# Jesus and Reincarnation

If Jesus had not been a reincarnationist, His entire message would have been fragmented, devoid of sure support, for lack of justice in its highest expression: to provide the transgressor a re-educational opportunity with the consequent growth toward freedom.

If the love He taught had not been anchored by the blessing of bodily rebirth giving rise to a new beginning and reparation, it would have had a transitory, sentimental nature, with the selection of the elect and fortunate to the detriment of the dislikeable and unfortunate.

Supported on the Doctrine of physical rebirth, He could immediately tell which needy persons were able to recoup or not recoup their health by taking into consideration the reasons for their suffering. Consequently, not all who asked for His help received it or were healed.

Since He knew it was actually the spirit that was infirm and not the body, He always addressed the individuality and not the personality with which people were clothed.

And since He understood human frailty, He emulated moral fortitude, true to the Law of Cause and Effect.

It was not only in His dialogue with Nicodemus that His statement about the *need to be born again* was implied.

It was repeated in various forms on other occasions, confirming the process of successive bodily experiences, the merciful gift of God's Love on behalf of all spirits.

In light of the widespread belief at that time in the plurality of rebirths, His disciples were not at all surprised by His response regarding *Elijah who had already come,* as well as His own question about who the people thought He Himself was.

✴

A pure spirit, He never became ill as He confronted the most diverse climactic and environmental factors with the same vigor and health, reflected in His countenance of comeliness and peace.

Whoever saw Him never forgot Him, and all those who felt His loving touch would stay forever imbued with His magnetism.

It is true that many who were partakers of His mercy did seem to forget Him... Nevertheless, they reincarnated down through history, bringing Him to the multitudes. Even today, they are engaged in making Him known and loved.

✴

His psychotherapy was based on reincarnation because He knew that individuals are the architects of their own destiny, living according to what they decreed through their past-life deeds.

That is why He never condemned anyone, whoever they might have been, and always offered them the chance to right their wrongs and be redeemed before their own conscience, as well as before the Divine Conscience.

Without favoring or disfavoring anyone or anything, He loved everything and everyone selflessly, embracing all humanity at all times in His ineffable affection.

He had sent missionaries throughout the earth, speaking the language of reincarnation, until He Himself came to confirm it, beckoning all with the hope of a blissful future.

*

Don't nail yourself to the cross of a guilty conscience after you realize your error.

Don't imprison yourself in *darkness* after you identify your offenses.

Don't feel overly distressed when you discover you were wrong.

*Rise* from the ashes and immediately start reparations, thus avoiding future expiatory returns, excruciating injunctions and pain-filled situations.

Ask for forgiveness and adopt a new approach regarding those whom you offended and harmed.

If they do forgive you, it will be good for all involved, but if not, understand them and move on, avoiding the same mistake.

If you have been wronged, forgive your offenders and detach yourself from them, offering them peace and experiencing the well-being that results from doing what is right.

Your reincarnation is a lofty gift that you must not waste.

Each moment is priceless for your endeavor of sublimation, detachment and the practice of pure love.

Shorten the number of your rebirths by acting uprightly and serving tirelessly and joyfully, for as He stated, to enter the Kingdom of Heaven – which extends from your conscience towards the infinite – "you must be born again."

# 3
# JESUS AND HUMANITY

Jesus-Man is the life lesson we draw from the Gospel as the invitation extended to the human being to become deified.

Not having created any doctrine or system, Jesus made His life a model for people to refine their humanness, taking it to a higher level.

In His time, and still today, humans have always been the symbol of violence, arrogance and presumptuousness, outward dominators yet bruised and battered in their fragility, conflicts and mortality.

After His example, a different human emerged: humble, uncomplicated, meek, yet strong in his or her spiritual immortality.

While the great thinkers of all times established doctrinal methods and systems, He anchored the pillars of humane ethics – essential for happiness – in love.

He did not use sophisms or syllogisms; He never resorted to eccentric behavior or complex formulas requiring high levels of intelligence or astuteness. All

His references were widely known, despite their new presentation.

He used a tiny *mustard seed* to teach about faith; fish and fishnets to leave indelible examples about work; seeds falling on different types of soil to demonstrate the diversity of human sentiments in relation to the luminous pollen of His word…

The *Sermon on the Mount* reversed what was conventionally accepted without discussion, praising the innocent victim instead of the arbitrary master; those hungry for justice, love and truth, rather than the rich, idle squanderers of life's resources.

※

Jesus is the historical figure most at one with the human being and humanity.

His entire ministry was about humanization, raising the instinctive individual to the realm of reason and, subsequently, to that of pure spirit.

Jesus is also the Man most at one with God.

He never referred to God as a distant, unknown or fearsome being.

He presented God as Love, loveable and knowable, close to human needs, compassionate and kind.

He reformulated and updated the Mosaic concept, rendering it attainable, drawing people closer to God, for God is always close to them, even when they refuse to give themselves to Him through love.

As for the *Kingdom,* He did not adorn it with chimeras or make it fearsome; instead, He awakened in hearts the desire to reach it in all its transcendence.

He denied the world without cursing it; He blessed it by acknowledging the wondrous landscape where He attended to the suffering, and He immersed Himself in profound meditation under the glittering stars of the Infinite.

Jesus is to humanity the light that warms and enlightens.

✶

If you have let yourself become fossilized by orthodox doctrines that claim Him as their founder, start anew and seek Him in the masses or in the silence of reflection, rereading His words without forged interpretations.

If you are disappointed with those who call themselves His followers but who do not live according to His examples, forget them. Be the one to follow Him in the simplicity of the invitations contained in the messages that He has been sending you to this day, and which remain as much alive as ignored.

If you have not yet felt His warmth, break the ice of your indifference and become at least somewhat impartial, without purposely preventing Him from entering your heart and mind.

In your present human condition, you need Him in order to grow and move beyond your limitations in the direction of His infinite love.

Indeed, Jesus came to humanize humankind.

Now it is up to you to leave your pettiness behind from time to time and receive Him, becoming Christ-like in the endeavor of your complete self-realization.

# 4
# Jesus and Love

The human figure of Jesus confirms His origin and accomplishments as the most perfect, complete Being that has ever walked the earth.

His entire life unfolded along the lines of profound oneness with the Divine Consciousness, while maintaining His individuality in perfect psychophysical balance.

Consequently, He inspired confidence due to His crystal clear character, which never submitted to the parameters of the time, characteristic of a primitive culture, in which moral corruption, hypocritical conservatism, arbitrary and prejudicial laws, and the formalistic preoccupation with outward appearances in detriment of authentic values predominated.

Bearer of authentic courage, He strove against injustice in every situation without fail, even when the general consensus condoned crime.

Patient and peaceable, He remained serene in the most adverse circumstances, and cheerful in emotionally charged moments, attesting to the completeness of His inner values in a rhythm of constant harmony.

In a violent, perverse society, He chose love as the solution to all matters at hand, and unrestricted forgiveness as the effective therapy for all infirmities.

He not only forgave through words, but mostly through clear and honest attitudes, putting Himself at risk by extending forgiveness especially to the unfortunate, the unclean, the outcast and the needy.

He never submitted to the damaging conventions of race, ideology, party or religion in detriment of unprejudiced and all-encompassing love for all.

\*

For love's sake, He chose a despised Samaritan as a *symbol of solidarity*.

For love's sake, He freed a wayward woman by removing her guilt complex.

For love's sake, He assisted the Syro-Phoenician foreigner who asked His help with her daughter's humiliating infirmity.[2]

His heart and hands were filled with love, to strew it over the downtrodden, whether a tax collector, an adulteress, a prodigal son, an impoverished widow or a mourning mother.

Love was always on His agenda, illuminating lives and assisting the needy in body, mind and soul.

\*

He showed mercy toward all; nevertheless, He held on to the energy that educates, uplifts, disciplines and saves.

---

[2] See Mark 7:24 ff. – Tr.

He wept over Jerusalem; He railed at the Pharisaical farce; He warned the wayward; He condemned hypocrisy and gave His own life in a sacrifice of love.

He never lost His way in childish sentimentality or hostility.

Love guided His steps, words and thoughts.

He became and still is the symbol of complete love for humankind, to which He promised a profound and liberating humanness.

# 5
# JESUS AND TOLERANCE

In terms of In-Depth Psychology, the issue of judging other people's wrongs is a seriously inhumane act toward the one who erred.

The problem of a *sin* belongs to the one who committed it, who afterward is subject to a painful process of self-punishment, seeking, even unconsciously, to break free of the wrong that, as guilt, weighs so heavily on the conscience.

Guilt is a perturbing *shadow* cast over the personality and is responsible for awful diseases that cause woes of various kinds.

Engraved on the innermost panels of the individuality, guilt automatically programs its own reparation processes.

Every heartless act practiced through arbitrary judgments generates, on its own accord, dynamics of future afflictions for accusers, themselves consciences bearing the weight of many problems.

Judging the actions of others as incorrect, accusers project their own *shadow* in the form of self-justification, which will not rid them of their own blemishes.

Consequently, tolerance for others and ourselves is a *sine qua non* personal and fraternal therapy that enables us to grasp the difficulties of those who err and offer them a helping hand.

As we accuse and judge others' wrongs, we yield to the dark trait of pleasure/vengeance in pointing out weaknesses in other people, who always deserve the same compassion that we would expect for ourselves in similar situations.

✳

Jesus was always very strict when teaching those who judged other people's behavior.

Of course, there are courts and appointed authorities in charge of the moral cleansing of society. They are responsible for catching and judging criminals, using re-educational means that are never punitive, because otherwise they would be guilty of identical, if not more serious crimes.

Judging the person is a manifestation of the ignorance of the causes of problems, and it demonstrates the moral primitivism of humans, who still act like *"wolves"* toward others.

The Master used an ingenious image for those who have *a plank* in their own eye yet *see a speck in the eye of their neighbor.*

The illustration is powerful in its inescapable clarity; it does not leave room for any evasion of responsibility.

When faced with the afflicted, wayward, wicked and maniacal multitudes, He did not judge them but was *taken with compassion* and helped them, instead.

Of course, He did not solve every problem or assist all those who wanted Him to. Nonetheless, He was compassionate and loved them, enveloping everyone in tenderness, always teaching the means of liberation to find peace.

✶

Have compassion on those who err. Their conscience will be their judge.

Help those who stumble. Their weakness is already their punishment.

Tolerate wrongdoers. They are your future, should you not be strong enough to proceed rightly.

Your tolerance toward the unfortunate will become the emotional measure of compassion you yourself will receive when your own time comes, for no one is blameless or perfect.

# 6
# Jesus and Honor

Jesus' psychic structure was the model of perfect oneness with the task He came to fulfill.

He grasped the fundamental laws of life that guided men and women, using words and actions to set a sure course for physio-psychological balance.

Although He was the personification of the Truth, He did not overwhelm others with His natural superiority, nor did He impose on their individuality, which became, if anything, more independent.

Those who grew fond of Him found peace; consequently, they freely chose to follow Him.

He knew how to awaken the individual's latent abilities and channel them for wholesome purposes, bringing happiness and completeness.

The parables, containing His living lessons, are still apropos for today's problems because their coherent meaning and guidance may be applied without any conflict of time, place or person.

✶

Modern people more or less continue to have the same aspirations and necessities as their ancestors, except for a few achievements over time.

For that reason, they still face needs and insecurities that perturb their emotional structure.

To attain inner emancipation, they need the light of knowledge and courage in order to honor themselves by decisively pursuing their objectives.

Knowing what one wants out of life and how to go about it – such is the birthing process of personal maturity, breaking with one's own atavistic roots carried over from one's spiritual past.

For this effort, honor becomes an unparalleled inner guide that propels one forward without delay.

When Jesus broke with the constraining ties to His family, albeit without neglecting His moral and social commitments to them, He demonstrated the greatness of His courage resulting from His personal honor.

When His family, unaware of His ministry and doubtful of His mission, came looking for Him hoping to interrupt His work of laying the foundations for the Good News in people's hearts, someone said to Him: *Your mother and brothers are here asking for You.*

The time had come for Him to make an unwavering yet honorable decision, allowing Him to ask calmly: *Who is my father, my mother, my brothers, except those who do God's will?*

Everyone's astonishment did not perturb Him. He carried on as if nothing had happened.

*

Honor is the courage to choose what is best.

Hesitating between those who wanted to hold Him back and those who needed His presence and lessons would mean the lamentable failure of His objectives.

There was no disrespect toward His family members, who, presumptuous, fearful, and not having previously consulted Him, disrespected His choice as an independent man that had come on a mission whose end He never denied: humiliation, the cross and death.

His honor led Him to carry on, even as He struggled against every hostile factor.

He had come to break down barriers, to wrest the modeled sculpture of the complete human being from the cold marble of a utilitarian and slavocratic society.

Honor was His chisel and duty was His hammer. Nothing could imprison Him within the limits of convention, childish fears or immature sentiments.

Twenty centuries later, He is still the same sculptor of souls, shaping the marble of lives in order to set them free.

*

Your honor should be molded on His.

Your decision for happiness, breaking with complacency and tradition, is your driving force.

Go within and scrutinize you conscience, your inner guide, in order to find out what you really want, what is best for you and how to get it.

Your liberation will be different than that which *breaks free* from a few sentimental bonds only to get caught in the grip of even worse situations.

The honor of finding an inner guide that teaches you about the fundamentals of a Jesus-centered life will break the shackles of everything holding you back so that you may press on.

Afterwards, you will never be the same, nor will you repeat yourself.

The awareness of duty will manifest in the honor of following standards of respect for everyone and everything, in complete freedom under Jesus' leadership.

# 7
# Jesus and Justice

The aim of Justice is to repair any damage caused by wrongdoers and to rehabilitate them, making them useful to society.

Justice works on education's behalf, using disciplinary measures that include limiting criminals' freedom in order to save them and the community from greater wrongs.

A crime results from disregard for established codes of law that govern peoples, providing individuals with equal rights and responsibilities.

Whenever Justice is corrupt, individuals act foolishly, and the abuse of authority leads to the extremes of wantonness.

In a just society, all enjoy equal opportunities for progress due to an equal distribution of wealth; the strong help the weak; the healthy assist the unhealthy; the young help the elderly – natural behavior resulting from a clear awareness of responsibility, which establishes happiness as a consequence of solidarity amongst diverse individuals.

As people develop their sentiments and intelligence, their laws become gentler and their justice more equitable.

In primitive cultures, the "law of the strongest" prevails, replaced later with the absurd condition of heredity, until more-elevated socio-democratic principles are reached, where personal responsibility takes priority in the freedom of the members.

However, the road is still long before respect for life, one's neighbor, nature and unarbitrary, non-punitive Justice is reached.

✻

Jesus was the champion of equitable justice.

His attitude toward people was always the same: benevolence with the aim of education.

He conceded to a meeting with Nicodemus, a doctor in the upper house of the Sanhedrin, as He did with Zacchaeus, a tax collector; He talked to Lazarus and his sisters in Bethany, as He did with the thief seeking His support on the cross.

Realizing that people differ due to their intellectual and moral achievements, and that their hierarchical level is the result of personal acquisition, without ostentation or privilege, He provided everyone with the same conditions, opportunities, and impartiality.

Whether to the adulteress, the prostitute, the priests who interrogated Him, the learned Sadducees, or the hypocritical Pharisees, He always granted the same treatment.

When He scolded those who tried to catch Him in their sophist, compromising snare, He was assertive without neglecting compassion, since He knew about their sickly soul, from which all behavior proceeds.

In an age of arbitrariness, He was magnanimous; of power abuse, He spoke about renouncing arrogance and becoming humble; of exploitation, He taught and lived benevolence.

He proposed that our justice should not be the "justice of the Pharisees," who, morally diseased, took advantage of the status quo by exploiting the weak, widows and children.

And when Pilate, who would *wash his guilty hands* due to the cowardice of his character, declared that he had power and authority over Him, Jesus stated that such power and authority had been granted, for even Pilate himself answered to a higher authority, since true power and perfect justice come from God alone.

*

If you are entangled in your own errors and caught in the web of incomplete human Justice, re-educate yourself!

If you are a victim of unfortunate circumstances weighing on you, trust in God and wait!

If you have been harmed and wrongly accused, do not despair!

Pay now what you forgot to pay yesterday, certain that the failure of earthly laws will not keep Divine Justice from reaching you.

It is better that you are repairing commitments that you do not remember than enjoying physical liberty while carrying a guilty conscience hidden in illusion.

True justice always finds the wrongdoer.

For your part, be just and equitable toward all, using as your model the behavior of Jesus, who never failed anyone.

# 8
# Jesus and Duty

There can be no doubt that countless people unconsciously believe they deserve to have it all. They even think the sun shines because they exist, in order to provide them with light, warmth and life.

They lock themselves up in their self-bestowed values, but when confronted with reality, they become embittered or rebellious and lapse into aggressiveness or depression.

They do not assume responsibility or fulfill their duties.

On occasion, they do make a commitment but soon abandon it, accusing others and feeling wronged.

They are demanding regarding other people's conduct, yet forgiving concerning their own errors.

Always in a state of confusion, they become a heavy burden on the social economy, creating unpleasant situations.

Easy-going and agreeable when esteemed, they become rude and thankless if not regarded as they think they should be.

Affable in success, they become aggressive when struggling.

They forget that life tests our courage, our morals, and that we all have non-deferrable duties toward it, our neighbor and ourselves.

No one has the right to enjoy something for nothing, exploiting someone else's efforts.

The prize is the honor conceded to the victor who has endeavored to achieve.

Step by step the traveler gains ground, gazing fixedly at the finish line.

Each person's duty guides him or her in the task of evolution.

This effort is the conscience's moral achievement once it becomes fully aligned with cosmic order.

Being useful in any and every circumstance, favoring progress, living with dignity – these are a few expressions of one's duty to life.

\*

In an unforgettable parable, Jesus delineated the behavior of a man who puts forth the effort to deserve respect, demonstrating his fragility, as well as his desire for self-renewal.

Matthew writes that *there was a man who had two sons*. He said to the first: *Son, go and work in the vineyard today,* to which the son responded: *Yes, sir;* but upon thinking it over, he decided not to go. He made the same request to the second son, who said: *I will not.* However, he felt bad and went. *Which of the two did the will of his father?* asked the Master. And His listeners answered: *The second.*[3]

In this experience, we are faced with action and promise, fact and intention.

---

[3] Matt. 21:28 ff. – Spirit Auth.

Action must predominate because it results from duty. For action, mellifluous or comforting words are not necessary, but rather the decision to proceed correctly.

Jesus always proposes duty, action; understand better to act better.

He never induces anyone to alienation from objective reality. He establishes a scale of values that must be respected, with the most relevant ones deserving priority, those that are essential accomplishments for upright individuals, who fulfill their duty.

Before Him, stagnation means death, and stagnation is a crime against the "Kingdom of God" lying within the human being and needing to be attained.

All the parables He offers us are action-packed, without external impositions, but rather the result of the lucid willingness of an awakened conscience.

✶

Never make a promise you do not intend to keep.

Never rest on your laurels. Assess the possibilities and press on.

The duty that imposes selflessness and hardship is the same that brings you harmony, ridding you of conflict and doubt.

Never cease to grow inwardly. The discontent you feel in regards to your accomplishments will be your motivation to aim higher.

You are a servant of the world.

Jesus, who came from the stars, stated that He was the servant of all so that *we may have life and have it abundantly.*

# 9
# Jesus and Joy

That sadness that dominates you, embittering your hours, is a serious illness that you must fight against starting right now.

Do not be complacent toward it or make any illusory justification for it. The arguments for unhappiness and dissatisfaction are nothing but sophisms and ways of avoiding reality.

Everyone has a myriad of problems. Without them, however, there would be no motivation to struggle, to progress.

That depressing longing that alienates and consumes you is a ruthless enemy, to which you freely give in without a fight, broadening its realm of control to the degree that you make room for it.

Whatever the cause may be, based on current events, you must transform it into a blessing that inspires you to reflection and not dismay.

Sadness is very toxic to the body and is a pestilence that destroys life.

Everything around you is a hymn of praise, joy and gratitude to God. Take a good look at it.

Only humans, as thinking beings, allow themselves to be smitten with sadness, slipping into heedless conflicts of rebelliousness.

∗

Sadness may be the result of two factors, among others: past recollections as a spirit, and perturbation due to obsessive repercussions.

In the first case, pessimistic feelings must be eliminated, forced out of the unconscious by way of new, pleasant and positive ideas, which you must cultivate and strive to fixate on your mental screens.

If you get used to thinking positively, you will overcome your bad memories.

Habits become engrained through repetition, controlling one's physical and mental automatisms.

In the second case, the mental and emotional hosting of malicious, discarnate spirits occurs because they are in tune with your mental wavelength, establishing a hypnotic hold that worsens over time.

In both cases, you are indebted to the sovereign Laws of Life.

However, you have not reincarnated only to *pay*, but rather to reimburse with love, freeing yourself of negative debts by way of appropriate action.

You are a candidate for reaching the summit; not a convict condemned to the galleys in the *shadows* of pointless remorse or wasted tears.

If you remain in your unhappy predicament, you are your own victim; but if you resolve to get out, you become your own psychotherapist.

✳

Only once did Jesus let Himself become sad and sorrowful: in Gethsemane, when He, alone, remained alert while His friends slept close by, despite the decisiveness of the penultimate hour. And He did it out of compassion for His unvigilant companions, who were unaware of the gravity of the moment.

He always cultivated the joy of hope, the blessing of health, the gift of peace.

His was a ministry of joyfulness, of transformation of the human being and the old world into an entirely new individual and society.

Rebirth is victory over death. It is the happiness that results from liberation.

Therefore, rend the shroud of *shadow* behind which you are hiding all your potential for victory. Go and sow fraternity in the great vineyard that awaits you.

Have a new, up-to-date self-encounter and examine yourself deeply without bemoaning your situation; then, head in the direction of success. This is fundamental, not as a payment but as a duty yet to fulfill for your recovery. God has granted you that right and you must respond to Him by taking advantage of it.

You probably suffer pressures resulting from people's lack of charity, but yielding to their restricting force is your own decision.

In fact, if you actually *do* want to leave sadness behind, you *can*. Otherwise, you are responsible because you enjoy it – this is a serious illness.

✸

"*Rejoice*," says Jesus, "*the Kingdom of God has come to you.*"

That *Kingdom* is within us, waiting to be discovered and inhabited.

It awaits you, unyielding. It has come to meet you where you are. Take a step in its direction; enter it; let yourself be filled with it; and rejoice always, as a hero who will finish the battle.

# 10
# Jesus and Courage

The courage of Jesus!

His life was one of constant challenge.

In continuous struggle for the Good, He never failed to act rightly, boldly.

The message He brought with the aim of freeing human minds for the Truth made Him the champion of courage.

He never concurred with wrongful conduct cloaked as lawfulness, arrogance masked as humility, injustice backed by the powerful, hypocrisy dressed up as honesty, or any sort of discrimination under social, economic, racial or religious justifications.

Even though Samaritans were detested and disregarded, He chose one as an example of solidarity rather than a presumptuous priest or a shrewd Levite, both enjoying some measure of prestige within the ruling community.

He lent His support to a woman who had made herself an object of pleasure, who was accused in public of having induced men to transgressions and crime, and He chose a disgraced woman to be a messenger of the good news of His resurrection.

He made Himself the voice of the humble and neglected, of those without rights or support so that their justifiable complaints would be heard.

He socialized with individuals of so-called "ill repute" without fear of contamination, and completely disregarded those who had ill-gotten privileges, to which they secretly surrendered.

He spoke gently to sufferers but emphatically and in a virile manner to wrongdoers, flatterers and cowards – whom He never feared.

He was never afraid about *losing* His life, because that is why He had come.

He did not negotiate favors or submit to human conventions.

He was humble, but never subservient; affable, but never sentimental; a friend, but never a subaltern.

Always stoic, He spoke and behaved appropriately for each occasion, person and circumstance, without straying from His itinerary.

He lived and acted firmly, without subterfuge; He behaved in only one manner: faithfulness to God.

✴

Lean on Him.

In times of trouble or otherwise, seek Him.

In harrowing doubt or persecution, consider how He would handle the situation and do as your upright conscience inspires you.

Serenely ponder Jesus' courage and follow His example.

Have the courage to live!

Do not bury your situation or furtively hide it behind excuses and lies.

Picture yourself bathed in the light of His teachings and break the shackles that bind you to fear, insecurity, instability, and mental/physical suffering.

Confident of victory, serenely confront your limitations and anxieties, and do not shirk your responsibilities.

Do not become depressed or remorseful with each failure, but learn how not to repeat it.

Experience is the summary of the attempts that have brought positive and negative results.

Never fear people by endowing them with a superiority and worth that they clearly do not have.

Do respect everyone's achievements, however; consider and use such examples for your own motivation so that you too may be just as successful.

Give yourself the right to be human and make it your duty to keep growing, without holding yourself back at your current level.

Always act with optimism.

Fear is an awful enemy that decimates lives by the millions.

✸

Courage is born in the moral values of people who choose upright conduct for a happy life.

The courage to live must be practiced constantly, overcoming the small obstacles of timidity, fear of failure, inferiority complexes and real or imaginary illnesses, strengthening the soul with each triumph and rethinking one's actions after each failure.

Courage is an achievement much different from recklessness.

Courageous people wait, believe and then act at the appropriate time, whereas reckless people act hastily, heartlessly and irresponsibly.

Use Jesus' courage as the example for your life and calmly press on.

# 11
# JESUS AND RESOLVE

To a young man who seemed ready to enter the New Era as a candidate to follow Him, Jesus proposed a direct invitation without preamble.

In spite of his eagerness, the young man balked, using the excuse that he needed to bury his deceased father first.

In answer to this seemingly justifiable response, the Master was blunt: *"Leave to the dead the care of burying their dead; but you, construct the Kingdom of God in your heart."*

Jesus' attitude and proposal to a son who only meant to fulfill his immediate duty seem strange, in this case, burying his discarnate father.

It is possible that this actually was his real intention, postponing his engaging the endeavor of life eternal; however, it is also possible that he was hiding some other intention.

✷

The desire to attend the funeral and burial of the dead body perhaps signified his concern with being seen as a faithful, loving son and therefore deserving of his inheritance.

Some testamentary disposition probably required him to carry out his final duty or else he would lose his inheritance, so his presence would not be an act of love but an ulterior motive.

Despite the usefulness of material possessions – they do promote comfort, progress and peace, if used rightly – at times they are cruel shackles, lifeless things that imprison people, and which, because they so often change hands, are dead things that do not deserve consideration in light of eternal truths.

✶

One might also guess that the young man, still avid for his youth, was unwilling to renounce it, using his excuse as a seemingly worthy way to avoid commitment.

Material pleasures are powerful chains that bind people to the primitive passions they must overcome for their own benefit, but which nearly always lead to moral decay and the death of ideals.

✶

Perhaps his concern for his new responsibilities caused the candidate unreasonable fear, which in turn led to his excuse.

The fear of taking on serious commitments prevents individuals from developing morally and intellectually, and keeps them stuck in the unconcerned, monotonous routines of their daily lives.

Jesus' invitation comes with an intense action plan that starts with inner renewal and continues in constructive activity for the Good everywhere.

Fear is the dissolving factor of human individuality. It is responsible for avoidable tragedies and crimes.

Fear is the driving force behind the death of dignifying achievements and of individuals themselves.

✷

Lastly, let us suppose that his filial love was, in fact, genuine and he really was concerned about his discarnate father.

Even so, any person could have buried the corpse, but no one except the young man himself could be responsible for his own illumination.

Jesus was his only chance.

Jesus probed him and knew the real reason for his refusal; nonetheless, He left him free to decide for himself.

The young man left to bury his father and never returned.

He missed his chance.

Many still do.

✷

Watch what you have chosen in your current existence: living to pursue the authentic existential objectives, or accumulating lifeless treasures only to bury them in the dust of oblivion.

Lay yourself bare on the inside and engage in soul searching.

What do you have that death cannot confiscate? What do you have that is real, that can follow you?

Be severe with this examination of your conscience and put yourself in the young man's shoes.
How would you have responded to Jesus?

✳

You complain and keep tabs on the problems afflicting you, ignoring or trying to ignore the fact that you are on the earth to learn, atone and reeducate yourself.

Look around and you will see how urgent your decision is for what is best and long-lasting as an immortal being.

If you put off making a decision, then when you finally do make it, the circumstances will not be the same and your situation will be different, perhaps complicated.

The time is now.

Let yourself be permeated with His presence and follow Him joyfully.

With that attitude your problems will look different; they will lose their stressful significance and will actually contribute to your happiness.

You will be reborn from the ashes to soar towards the Great Light, overcoming the unnerving night.

# 12
# Jesus and Responsibility

As social beings, humans possess an inherent powerful mechanism that makes them want to avoid responsibility. Thus they attribute their failures to other people, fate, the circumstances of their birth, or even God.

Or, as an alternative, they develop a guilt complex and sink into depression, in which they hide their childishness, regardless of their age.

Responsibility is the result of a discerning conscience that grasps the reason, purpose and aim of one's life, working to assume the role for which one is destined.

For this reason, responsible persons are neither neglectful nor hurried. With the goal of achieving wholeness, they implement a serene action plan within the parameters that characterize individual and collective progress.

Responsible people know what to do, when to do it and how to go about it.

They do not become social parasites, ride on other people's success or hide behind silly excuses.

Their lucidity is extremely valuable to their social group. Due to the natural security they provide, their presence may go unnoticed, but their absence is always felt.

Responsibility drives people to the extremes of sacrifice, self-denial and the renunciation of their well-being, even their lives.

✸

As the shepherd of souls, Jesus has taken responsibility for us, enlightening us regarding our duties, true needs and real objectives.

Furthermore, He gave Himself for us even in death, as if His life by itself were not a great and stoic enough sacrifice of love.

Nevertheless, He called all those who sought Him to the duty of responsibility, which renders them capable of great achievements.

Knowing the human soul in its full reality, He identified it as the source of all ills as well as all blessings.

Because people actually cling to their woes for the pleasure they bring, they become inured to their misfortune, in which they remain somewhat comfortable, despite their display of discomfort and unhappiness.

Consequently, aware as He was of the causes of their troubles, whenever Jesus received those who came to Him, He strongly urged them not to return to their erroneous ways so that something even worse would not befall them.

✸

Responsibility frees people from themselves, lifting them to the higher planes of life.

As long as they insist on cultivating primitive passions, they misadjust their emotional structure, becoming their own victims and falling prey to degenerative and caustic illnesses.

Moral renewal provides an effective channel for wholesome energies, preserving individuals for the higher purposes for which they are destined.

✸

Humankind has survived thanks to its responsible individuals, who work continuously for the Good, the Beautiful and the Ideal.

They stand out for the greatness of their accomplishments, cemented in personal sacrifice.

✸

After He healed lepers, obsessed individuals, and the woman caught in adultery, Jesus' warning to them was always based on responsibility so that, in storing up ethical values and fulfilling spiritual duties, they would not return to their wrongful ways.

✸

Right now, as you need Him, reformulate your notions about life and begin to act correctly, led by responsibility. Do not blame others for your setbacks and failures. Identify them and begin your renewal.

Even if you do not want it, you are nonetheless always responsible for the consequences of your actions.

You will reap what you sow.

Therefore, assume your commitment to the Master and you will stay healthy inwardly, uprightly pursuing your duties with responsibility.

# 13
# Jesus and Revolution

Jesus always acted as a profound psychologist. People's outward appearance, the way they spoke about their illnesses, or their sentiments were not important to Him.

✳

When people talk about what is going on inside them, they invariably use words to hide what they would otherwise like to say.

People have an unconscious dread of laying themselves bare to themselves, let alone to someone else.

On the other hand, very few people know how to listen, see and understand.

A friendly smile at one moment may become a sneer the next, and kindness may turn into violence.

Furthermore, listeners receive speakers' projections, adapting the information to their own predicament, and their grasp of it to their own areas of conflict.

As the Perfect Man, Jesus, clear in His effective transparency, penetrated people's deepest, unconscious mysteries, with which they struggled on the surface of effects without going back to the causes.

His dialogues were short and to the point.

He used neither circumlocutions nor evasions.

When He spoke in parables or used a question to answer a question asked by hypocrites and Pharisees, He was employing unparalleled techniques, by which such imposters revealed themselves in their own words.

He did this repeatedly. He used it with the priest who asked Him who his neighbor was, which resulted in the Parable of the Good Samaritan, leading the priest, through logic, to the conclusion. Likewise, He applied the method with those who asked Him if it was lawful to pay taxes, requesting a coin and asking them whose likeness was engraved on it.

*

It was with sufferers, however, that He employed the best psychotherapy anyone has ever known.

He did not probe His patients' dreams to discover their unconscious, their archives and their psychological *shadows*.

He did not prescribe the usual medications or other complex formulas.

He did not attribute their guilt to their family, heredity or socio-economic factors.

He did not make them somatize their stressful issues through accusations of any sort.

Instead, He loved them; offering them safety and helping them rediscover their latent, abandoned abilities.

He awakened in them a new vision of life, supporting them at that moment, but not keeping them from continuing, as they so desired.

He never imposed Himself on anyone.

All sought Him, whereas He sought no one, because the success of any undertaking depends on the interested party. The circumstantial factors are the arena, the space where they will act.

✳

It is true that nearly all those who benefitted by receiving His liberating light pressed on alone by personal choice.

Many, if not most, were ungrateful; others fell back into the same web of indolence that made them weak in the first place; many others unconsciously and inadvertently accused Him. None, however – without exception – were immune to His magnetism, His affability and His power.

A revolutionary par excellence, He turned the struggle inside out: the death of the "old man" and the birth of the "new man."

He offered the first step – it was up to the candidate to take the rest.

The endeavor was general; the action of each one was each person's responsibility.

Pressing on, He prepared the road.

The enemies were on the inner battlefield of each combatant.

He also knew that the effort was arduous and that only perseverance, time and toil would lead to victory. Thus, He never became irritable or impatient.

✳

If you really do want to be cured of your ills, allow yourself to be scrutinized by the Sublime Psychotherapist.

Follow His instructions.

Revolutionize yourself by breaking from self-indulgence, self-punishment, self-pity and the dark past.

Be reborn on the inside.

If you want true victory, get on the battlefield and fight. Open yourself up to love, and love without expecting a response.

You are not alone in the battle.

Like you, other combatants await support.

Find out who they are and join forces with them, knowing, however, that your revolution is in connection with Jesus; it is not against the world, humankind or life.

# 14
# Jesus and Possessions

The attachment to material things becomes a cage that imprisons distracted owners, who actually end up belonging to that which they think they possess.

Possessions cause affliction due to the fear of losing what has been accumulated, the anxiousness to pile up even more, and having to leave them when ever-present death draws nigh.

Possessions foster delusion because they intoxicate individuals with pride and power, believing they deserve privileges and exceptional deference, which do not keep them from becoming ill, neurotic, lonely and dying like everybody else.

Possessions harden the sentiments, which lose the tonic of solidarity, compassion and charity, causing one to forget about others and think only of oneself.

They elicit the presumption that one was born to be served, abandoning the spirit of service that dignifies and favors progress.

Owners who are not interested in sharing values or offering worthy opportunities for work are slaves who become more and more tarnished as their attachment to their possessions intensifies.

✶

Wealthy are all those who give, spreading their wealth, which multiplies in various hands for the general good.

Truly wealthy people are conscious investors who do not hinder society's growth, but broaden its arena of accomplishments.

They know they are temporary stewards and not permanent owners and that, when the time comes, they will have to render an accounting for the wealth that was entrusted to them.

Actually, people own nothing at all – neither themselves, nor their lives; they merely use whatever comes and goes. Discovering this reality harmonizes them inwardly and with all that is temporary while in transit to what is eternal: their spiritualization.

Eventually they enjoy wealth but do not hold on to it; as for life, they no longer abuse it.

✶

Jesus' encounter with the rich young man who was ready to follow Him is clothed with remarkable present-day content.

In spite of having fulfilled the formal requirements of society and religion, he was unaware of how important it was to align his life with the fertile ideal of life eternal.

He wanted the "Kingdom" while enjoying the favors of the world in the form of assets that made his opulent journey easy.

He longed to follow Jesus and enjoy His company without contributing anything in return.

Acquiring more without depriving himself of anything was his plan.

✷

The Master, who knew him deeply, established, as the fundamental requirement, that he sell all he possessed, give the money to the poor and then follow Him.

✷

Life entails exchanges and trade-offs.

*To those who have, it will be given, and from those who do not have, it will be taken* - from those who are miserly and never share the excess, it is nothing, but to everybody else, it is everything.

The young man was rich and hedonistic but he was not happy, because he lacked solidarity, which pacifies the anxieties of the heart.

Perhaps, he could have freed himself from material things; however, he was not used to the limits of want, to making ends meet, or to a less preeminent position, lacking the deceitful attraction of vanity and flattery.

Renouncing his wealth would have been a step in the direction of self-denial, and that was too much for him.

Blessed with abundance, he dreaded lack.

Thus he rejected what was permanent and lost himself in banality.

※

Along with your money, properties, securities and livestock, you also possess, as tormenting assets, the passions and caprices resulting from them.

You long for peace and love, happiness and self-realization; nevertheless, when the opportunity arises, you hesitate and calculate what you must give in exchange, choosing to continue as you always have.

You desire, but feel unsure about the choice you have to make, the contribution you must offer and your struggle for liberation.

Happiness only exists for those who are free.

There is happiness only for those who, having found the truth, assimilate it and take it as their norm of conduct.

※

In the whirlpool of your squabbles and conveniences, if you long for a new and harmonious life, listen to Jesus: *Rid yourself of everything, give to others what may be useful, and follow me.*

Unburdened, you will be blessed by the light, and, consequently, be free and happy.

# 15
# Jesus and Torments

Generically speaking, human beings have been considered to be a still-incomplete mental and physical mass heading for the grave, where it decays.

Religions say that the soul has a destiny purposefully fixed in the future, reposing in idleness or suffering everlasting punishment.

For the former, the world is a place of immediate pleasures with the unavoidable presence of suffering, which is part of its imperfection; for the latter, it is a "valley of tears" or a "place of exile."

On the one hand, the simplistic information of nothingness after death; on the other, pre-set fatalism, violating the codes of wanting, struggling and overcoming.

Either one of these currents of thought unavoidably leads to torment.

Here, pleasure until the senses grow numb; there, frustrating bitterness, the banishment of happiness in evasion of reality dynamics.

Based on these two aspects, there are those who live to enjoy and those who deny themselves any form of enjoyment.

✳

Jesus was the prototype of happiness.

He loved nature, people and the simple endeavors with which He wove His wonderful parables.

He neither condemned nor praised earthly conditions.

As Master, He taught how one should utilize and respect them, using their means to generate happiness for all, thus honoring them.

As a Physician of souls, He prescribed experiencing them without becoming enslaved, pointing to loftier goals to be reached through personal effort.

✳

Human torments proceed from a guilty conscience.

Originating from other bodily existences, the spirit inherits its own actions, which resurface as effects.

When the effects are healthy, they are beneficial; the opposite is equally true.

From the deep archives of the individuality arise matrices of afflictions that surface as purifying processes, facilitating the onset of illnesses, torments and dissatisfaction.

Likewise, they create appropriate conditions for an easy or arduous life in the home either characterized by socio-economic and moral problems or enriched with love and resources that favor one's journey.

Within the profound, immortal soul lie the roots of the phenomena that now sprout in the soil of the physical body.

✳

Your current torments are torments you engendered in past lives.

You ruthlessly tormented others, and now you suffer without comfort.

You mercilessly afflicted others, and now you hurt without affection.

You troubled others with perversity and now you trouble yourself without consolation.

Your inner being is a boiling caldron.

Conflicts follow conflicts, and you move in desperation from one to the next.

It is hard for you to exteriorize and talk about them in order to feel relief.

Phobias, complexes and repression dominate your mental landscape and you feel like a failure.

Re-temper your soul, however, and leave the den of your torments for the clear light of reason.

No one on this earth is destined for suffering or destructive conflicts.

All return to learn, recover and rebuild.

In the absence of love-action, suffering-renewal appears.

Therefore, pursue peace and release from your distress, and you will soon experience them.

✳

In the unforgettable encounter between Jesus and the woman of loose morals, who washed His feet with the ointment of her tears and wiped them with her hair, we find the psychotherapy for all miseries.

Jesus said to His host, who mentally criticized Him for condoning the attitude of the poor, wretched woman: *"She has loved much; consequently, her sins shall be forgiven."* Looking at her with tenderness and affection, He instructed: *"Go in peace; your faith has saved you."*

Love that has been converted into reparation for one's wrongs is the effective remedy for all the sores of body, mind and soul.

Love and be at peace, leaving your pain in the past; and arising from the rubble, resurface, happy, for a sound reconstruction of your life.

# 16
# JESUS AND REST

Within human beings there is an immense, ever-present desire to rest, to unwind, to stop working, to recharge one's energies.

Yearly vacation plans ensue with trips, sports and entertainment.

Those who live in the country want to travel to the city; those who work in the mountains want to go to the beach; those who live in the tropics long for the cold; and vice-versa.

Travel *fever* has a strong grip on people.

Those who do not get to travel feel diminished, marginalized, lacking social *status*.

Furthermore, all desire to fulfill their alternative plan of unwinding and resting.

Many people work at exhausting jobs throughout the year in order to save money to fulfill their *dream* of taking a vacation.

They toil until they are worn out; they go in debt and pay exorbitant, crippling interest later so they can enjoy today.

They talk about how easy it is to travel and its advantages, but it is all just words.

It is a type of fad.

But with rare exceptions, trips are painful and outings exhausting. There is precious little rest and a lot of inconvenience. As the days pass, the initial happiness and enthusiasm wither eventually and are replaced by irregular sleep, bad moods, unending hours in crowded hotels with bad service, and other drawbacks.

Attractive advertisements paint a rosy picture but the reality is very different.

And even if the usual problems do not occur, travelers, upon returning, compose themselves in order to impress those who did not go, and embellished stories flow from the smiling lips of the lucky ones, who must now return to their toil to cover the expenses, becoming even more tired than before.

*

Every change of activity fosters the renewal of one's energies and provides new motivation.

A good balance of endeavors defines what options are available as alternatives for well-being.

Of course, people need vacations, rest and entertainment, which provide them with joy and renewal to continue their work.

However, exciting, exorbitant plans, continuous activity and pre-set schedules are unnecessary and a waste of energy.

Preoccupation with clothes, appearance and the torment of shopping for novelties and souvenirs wear on the nervous system, which falters, causing irritability and a bad mood.

✼

Jesus said that *The Father works even today,* and that He, Jesus, *works also.*

Labor is a law of life as is rest. However, rest does not mean idleness or chasing after pointless things.

Rest means inner tranquility, recovery of one's strength, optimism, and feeling good about life.

Providing oneself with relaxation, pleasant reading, healthy sports, spending time with experienced, jovial, happy persons in quietude, and traveling serenely to discover other places, customs and people, without haste – all these are an effective means for a well-utilized rest.

Likewise, meditating in one's own home; praying, seeking to attune oneself with the founts of superior thought; fraternizing with sufferers, consoling and assisting them; being at peace, listening to melodies of deep emotional content – all these are invaluable resources and rest techniques that can be used anywhere whenever possible.

Just *go into your room, shut the door* and talk to God, as Jesus taught regarding prayer. The *room* is your inner world, and the *door* is the access to the outside. In that silent place you will hear God.

✼

In your physical and mental health program, include rest as a necessary priority.

But be mindful of what you opt for as a means of rest.

Use the occasion to discover yourself, to know yourself better and to identify what is actually indispensable to you, carefully selecting what you really need for a healthy life, abandoning or giving less importance to all else.

Yes, rest with spiritually uplifting activity.

# 17
# Jesus and Insecurity

On the earth, security is very difficult to achieve. Since earth is "a planet of trial and expiation," evolution always demands arduous efforts in the struggles that all have to face.

Likewise, the fragile body, subject to the many things that assail it, provides only temporary states of harmony because it is altered by wear, imbalance and continuous renewal of its parts.

From the emotional point of view, the inheritances latent in the spirit, responsible for its growth, surface and resurface as anguish and joy, succeeding each other until the moment of liberation.

Furthermore, people's moral level has not allowed them to break free from their aggressive instincts, which cause neuroses, paranoia, mental illnesses and violence.

Consequently, wrongs overwhelmingly increase while the dynamics of repression also become merciless, making the whole world an immense arena in which antagonistic forces incessantly battle one another.

The markets for sex, drugs and vice in general have driven populations to insanity, and insecurity has become almost the normal state of affairs.

Everybody tries to get used to it and live with it, almost expecting a personal attack at any time.

Distrust has set in and a whole string of omens has followed, gradually dominating people's psychological landscape.

*

Understanding the primitive state in which the humanity of His time struggled, Jesus knew how difficult it would be to instill peace in people's hearts and how many tears would have to be shed for that to happen.

That is why He foresaw the catastrophes and hecatombs people would unleash, as well as the countless afflictions they would impose on themselves as they slowly learned to respect life – according to what His disciple wrote in the *prophetic sermon*.[4]

However, He offered a peaceful vision when He stated that *those who persevere until the end shall be saved.*

In that context, salvation is to be understood as a state of tranquil conscience, of self-discovery, in which the inner world looms, governing the dysfunctional impulses and harmonizing the individual.

Saved are those who know who they are, what they have come here for, and how to accomplish it, thus confidently going about fulfilling their commitment.

Responsibility provides them with relative security for carrying out their activities.

---

[4] Mark 13:1 ff. – Spirit Auth.

Each person has a specific commitment in and toward life. Jesus demonstrated it; His was building the *Kingdom of God* on earth.

He never stalled, nor did He ever postpone that achievement.

Likewise, personal and collective security is the result of the level of the individual's and social group's commitment.

He attested to His security at every moment by being unrestrictedly committed.

He proposed: *"Do you believe in God? Believe also in me; Go and preach; Take my burden upon you and learn from me, for I am gentle and humble of heart…"*

His commitment to the Truth often revealed the security that sustained Him in His endeavors.

Never aggressive or stubborn, His certainty was serene, His determination unshakable.

The Master's security calmed those He supported, those who trusted in Him.

Always serene, He radiated security, which spread to all those who surrendered to Him, even as they courageously faced martyrdom.

✷

Jesus teaches how people are to strive for their mental evolution, alongside their physical evolution, both of which take time. Consequently, He did not offer a simplistic or salvationist recipe. Instead, He proposes maturation by constant effort through advances and setbacks to instill the learning experience and proceed until reaching the ultimate goal.

Knowing how to wait in sustained effort is a law that leads to victory.

*

As you desire security in your life, seek Jesus and entrust your plans to Him.

Do your part and do not give up on achieving seemingly distant objectives.

Take heart and persevere.

Security will come to you as an effect of the peace that will illumine your heart, serving as a stimulus for all your future achievements.

# 18
# Jesus and Suffering

Whenever the ill and infirm approached Jesus, He always asked them if they really wanted to be healthy and if they believed He could heal them.

It was of fundamental importance to reestablish their inner security about those two requisites: wanting and believing.

Since they complement each other, they are essential for the physical and mental reestablishment of the person desiring to be healed.

✽

Wanting intensely, unreservedly, completely alters people's psycho-physical picture from one of imbalance to one of balance, thus helping the organism restore its damaged areas.

Illness is nothing more than a *symptom* of the disarrangement of the spirit, the illness's actual bearer.

The act of wanting frees it from pernicious elements, generators of disturbances that surface in the emotions, mind and body.

Wanting means deciding, abandoning parasitical complacency or the fear of assuming new responsibilities in relation to life, thereby breaking the chains of persistent rebelliousness, self-pity and the *shadows* in which the individual hides.

Those who want, invest; and to invest, they act in a way to reap the desired results.

✴

Believing is a serious decision, one of emotional and human maturity.

Belief lives innate in the individual, waiting for stimuli that enable it to blossom, injecting life with additional forces.

There is an automatic, natural belief – the archetypical inheritance of past generations – which induces one to accept facts, ideas and experiences without analyzing them rationally. And there is another kind of belief, which is the result of logical development, of evidence based on events to which reason gives its assent.

Therefore, one believes based on both instinct and experiential knowledge.

✴

When one wants to be free from doubt, the belief in one's success is implicit in the desire.

Fear does not gain a foothold and hesitation does not produce a lack of confidence.

The mental landscape glows with light and the components of unhappiness dissolve under the powerful rays of a well-directed will.

✳

Wanting and believing lead to struggle, due to the decision to exit the shadowy cave for the arena of success.

After the happy achievement, those two moral values must continue to command one's emotional integrity in order to avoid a relapse.

✳

As was the case in several other incidents, in the one involving the paralytic lowered through the roof to the Master's presence, two issues were involved.

To the direct question: *Do you believe I can heal you?* the lame man answered: *Yes,* demonstrating his faith, while at the same time showing, due to the effort he put forth to be there, that he wanted to regain his health.

He had set friends and sympathetic persons in motion; he had submitted to the discomfort of being carried there; he had increased his pain, and because he wanted, he was successful.

Touched by such effort, Jesus freed him from his infirmity.

✳

In your difficulties and suffering, abandon your complacency about them and make the firm decision to want to be happy and then believe that you can actually be happy.

Nothing is keeping you from trying. All you have to do is establish inwardly the strong desire for release.

If you are hounded by doubt, rebuff it.

If you are perturbed by pessimism, remember those who have triumphed before you.

Their efforts for victory were no different.

It was just that they began their endeavors without your being aware of it, and now you see only the result.

Lastly, firmly appeal to Jesus, certain that your prayer will be answered. Open yourself to the influx of His restorative energy without erecting barriers.

If you want peace and health, and if you believe they can be realized right away, do not put off your moment to acquire them, for it is now.

# 19
# Jesus and Ingratitude

The sentiments of love, justice, charity and gratitude are inherent in human nature, natural heir of the good, the noble and the beautiful. However, because human nature is still lagging in the acquisition of its values and is more connected atavistically to the primitive instincts, these qualities do not manifest and must be cultivated with effort until they are automatically expressed as a result of one's inner evolution.

Consequently, the troubling manifestations of aggressiveness, rebelliousness and ingratitude are more common, maintaining a bellicose emotional and mental climate amongst humans.

Ingratitude, a form of contempt, is a serious imperfection of the soul and needs to be corrected.

Ingrates are sickly individuals that burn in the flames of badly disguised pride and perverse dissatisfaction. They attribute all rights and merits to themselves, denying the benefactor the least consideration and acknowledgement.

They quickly forget the good that was done to them and keep quiet about it, even when they think that what they received was simply what was owed to them, although insufficient for their level of importance.

Ingratitude is a festering moral sore in the individual that debilitates the surrounding social organism.

Thus, ingrates are numerous; they are always proud and *self-sufficient*, although morbidly dependent on the sacrifices of others.

\*

Jesus always admonished the ingrates that crossed His path.

There was never a lack of such unfortunate individuals in His ministry.

When He healed the ten lepers, their ingratitude was obvious, and when one of them did return to thank Him, He asked: *"Where are the others? Were not ten healed?"*

Nine of them had rushed off, healed on the outside but not yet free from disease on the inside. Inner healing would only happen when they became thankful, thus changing both psychologically and morally.

During the tragedy on Calvary, not one of the many whom He had healed was present.

He had illumined sightless eyes; He had opened deaf ears; He had provided sound to silent lips; He had given balance to delirious minds; movement to dead limbs; life to cataleptics; physical healing to bearers of countless maladies, and yet, He was forgotten by all of them. In spite of the good they had received and failed to acknowledge, the ingrates were faced with themselves, with consciences afflicted with remorse, becoming infirm again and dying, for no one escapes that biological phenomenon.

✶

The Master understood people's moral weaknesses. He was always concerned about reaching such weaknesses so that His healing would reach the origins of the infirmities, eradicating them such that they would not return to produce miasmas and perturbing ills.

He constantly suggested the renewing of goals, attitudes and thoughts.

As the supreme example, He asked that they come to Him, that is, that they follow His example of detachment from caustic passions and focus on *just one necessary thing*: the *Kingdom of God* in the heart.

In their search for what is most important, encountering it eliminates what is secondary – which ceases to have value – to give way to what is essential and necessary.

In the superficiality of their interests, however, people only yearn for immediate gratification, which ends up producing even more anxiety.

Due to their spiritual immaturity, they cut down the tree from which they picked fruit today, naively believing they will not be hungry tomorrow. But when they are, their source of nourishment is gone.

That is how ingrates act.

They cloud the water source that quenched their thirst; they burn the wheat that gave them bread; they cut the plant that fed them; they abandon the generous friend that helped them.

In return, they live alone, wretched inwardly because they know who they really are.

Distrustful, they become neurotic; unpredictable, they are unloved; proud, they are ignored.

*

Do not concern yourself with ingrates on your paths of love.

Press on, offering light without being troubled by the stubbornness of the darkness.

Wherever you turn on a lamp, its light will pour out gifts.

The beneficiaries that have forsaken or forgotten you, or who have turned on you, will learn from experience later on and will understand what they have done.

They will remember your attitude and will pass on what they received from you.

Therefore, it is not important what they do in return, but what you keep on doing for them.

# 20
# Jesus and Enemies

While technological progress has provided people with comfort, it relentlessly equalizes people at the same level, producing a sort of dehumanizing equality that consumerism has established as an important social achievement.

In fact, a community is regarded as happy due to the electronic devices, automobiles, yachts and airplanes available to it.

Fads rage, causing *copy-cat* behavior, where people imitate one another, assuming identical postures, with a weakening of ideals, ethics, family and the individual per se.

In reaction to such conduct, there are an increasing number of those who present themselves as original – the counterculture – who are no longer shocking with their exoticism and scorn of everything and everyone. Readily accepted and imitated at first, they are quickly discarded once the novelty wears off.

Such postures hide so-called *collective complexes,* which destroy life by installing a climate of indifference, if not instability in people.

There are models for all types of individuals with unjustifiable contempt for their human identity.

Suffocated by the lack of humaneness and afraid of confronting themselves, people seek refuge in political parties, social and sports clubs, and various clusters.

They stay in the crowd but suffer unbearable loneliness.

They see enemies everywhere and try to avoid them, using various types of segregationist artifices, all the while hiding behind a democratic and supportive facade.

✶

The cruelest enemies, however, lie within individuals themselves. They give them life and strength through pride, selfishness and the disguise of apparent social convention.

Jesus knew how to identify them as no one has ever managed to do in such depth.

He listened to those who approached Him, even though they tried but failed to hide their real motives.

Hypocrites and deceivers were laid bare before His piercing vision.

His moral position overwhelmed them and He confronted them either with love or vehemence, depending on the circumstance and their intention; but He was always benevolent.

He taught each one to go within and scrutinize him or herself in order to root out the unfolding webs of evil.

Immediately afterwards He would encourage them to grow personally by dismantling the mental and social dynamics that were conspiring for widespread decadence due to the drop in the cultural and emotional level that should comprise the foundation of society.

✳

Peter's thrice-repeated denial of his Friend serves as a powerful lesson, for as soon as he came to his senses, he *wept bitterly*.[5]

The explosion of tears was a cathartic chance for him to free himself from the remorse that could have rendered him neurotic and led him, like Judas, to the shame of taking his own life.

He rose from his downfall and defeated his enemies – fear and cowardice – to spend the rest of his life striving to make amends through practicing the Good.

Jesus, in turn, accepted his offering of love and utilized him in His ministry.

The Master knew Peter. That is why He predicted his defection and weaknesses, pointing out the inner enemies against which Peter would have to struggle.

✳

Do not be afraid to confront your *shadows,* those enemies stirring within you.

Be strong and focus on Jesus, the proper therapist.

Let your emotion reach Him.

Do not fear the adversaries with which you unconsciously live.

Identify them one by one and then unburden yourself of their pressure on you.

Recover your humanity and be yourself.

---

[5] Matt. 26:75 – Spirit Auth.

Mix in with everyone in your social group but preserve yourself by not giving in to the impositions of devouring and neurosis-producing consumerism.

Be open to renewal, diversity and your self-identity.

Unburdened of perturbing preventions and precautions, you will enjoy optimism, an essential factor for a healthy life and wholesome social relationships.

Made in the USA
Middletown, DE
04 May 2019